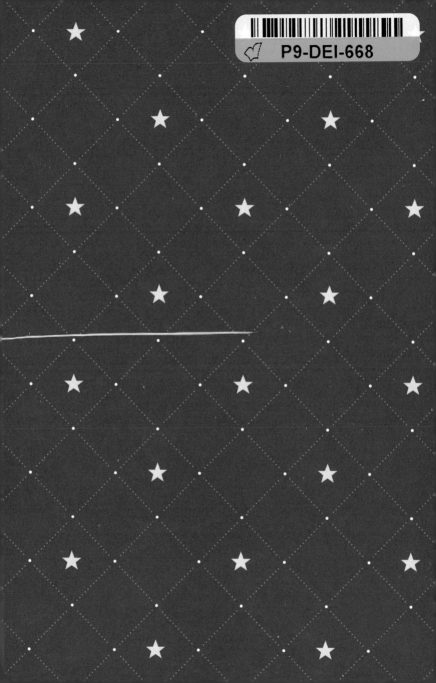

....

TO

....

FROM

....

DATE

NGRESS, JULY 4, 1776.

laration of the thirteen united States of America.

Published in Nashville, Tennessee, by Thomas Nelson. Thomas Nelson is a registered trademark of HarperCollins Christian Publishing, Inc.

Thomas Nelson titles may be purchased in bulk for educational, business, fund-raising, or sales promotional use. For information, please e-mail SpecialMarkets@ThomasNelson.com.

ISBN: 978-0-7180-3250-0

Printed in the United States of America

16 17 18 19 RRD 5 4 3 2 1

www.thomasnelson.com

IF MY PEOPLE

JACK COUNTRYMAN

COUNTRYMAN

A Division of Thomas Nelson Publishers

THOMAS NELSON
Since 1798

Contents

Freedom Is Never Free

Throughout the history of our country, men and women have been called to make great sacrifices and give their time and sometimes their very lives, that we might enjoy freedom, liberty, and the pursuit of happiness. With every challenge we have faced, we have risen to defend the nation we love and cherish.

Today we find ourselves facing many of the same challenges of our forefathers. We have been at war with those who wish to destroy our land and jeopardize our religious freedom for many years. We find ourselves at the crossroads of determining the direction of our country's future and the role of Christianity in our nation.

★
★★

The devoted prayers of all Americans will impact the future direction of our beloved country. Our prayer is that this book will draw you closer to our heavenly Father as you commit yourself to pray for our country.

★ ★ God Bless America! ★ ★

Freedom has its life in the hearts, the actions, the spirit of men and so it must be daily earned and refreshed— else like a flower cut from its life-giving roots, it will wither and die.

—DWIGHT D. EISENHOWER

The Power
of Prayer

Since our nation's very first days, God's greatest movements in our midst have been fashioned and sustained by prayer, from the signing of our earliest documents, to our triumphs over days of darkness, to the spiritual awakenings that have sustained our faith and resolve over the centuries. Throughout Scripture and throughout our history as a nation, persistent, prevailing, intentional, and never-ending prayer has always brought the presence of God.

How vast are the possibilities when we pray! Prayer is a wonderful power placed by the almighty God into the hands of His saints. When we humbly seek His face in prayer, He is moved to act on our behalf and accomplish His desires for us.

And when we seek God in prayer for our leaders, we impact the very direction our nation will take. This forty-day prayer journey is designed to help quicken your prayers, to encourage you to seek God's will for our future and ask Him to continually intercede on behalf of our nation. Prayerfully seek His face every day, believe that your prayers are making a difference, and claim all victory that is and is to come! For there is tremendous power in prayer.

We the People

DAY 1

Father,

We seek Your sovereign blessing on our nation. Forgive us for our shortcomings and the times when we have failed You. Draw us back to Your love and strengthen us as a nation to serve and honor You in all that we do. May we forever be faithful to the calling that You have given us. We respectfully and humbly give thanks for Your continued blessing.

If My people who are called by My name will humble themselves, and pray and seek My face, and turn from their wicked ways, then I will hear from heaven, and will forgive their sin and heal their land.

2 CHRONICLES 7:14

"Hear, O My people, and I will admonish you!"

PSALM 81:8

G od desires that this great nation will turn to Him, read His Word, and obey His commands for the good of our country. Throughout history God has faithfully led us through trials, wars, economic crises, and social issues coming to a boil. Every time He has seen us through and blessed our land far more than we deserve. Let us always seek the Lord for His direction for our blessed land.

DAY 2

Lord,

You have asked us to call to You, with the promise that You will answer when we do. We humbly seek Your guidance for our nation. Give us wisdom so that we will be a people filled with Your presence and guided by Your Spirit. Help us, O Lord, to honor You in word and deed, that we as a people will have Your blessing and favor.

"Call to Me, and I will answer you, and show you great and mighty things, which you do not know."

JEREMIAH 33:3

I have called upon You, for You will hear me,
*   O God;*
Incline Your ear to me, and hear my speech.

PSALM 17:6

Because He has inclined His ear to me,
Therefore I will call upon Him as long as
*   I live.*

PSALM 116:2

The Bible encourages us to call upon the Lord in every situation in our lives and, by extension, in our land. Our God who never sleeps will hear our prayers 24/7. So it only seems right that one duty of every Christ-following person blessed to live in this country is to pray for this nation. The One we call to has promised to listen.

The Bible and the American Presidents

The Bible is the one supreme source of revelation of the meaning of life, the nature of God, and spiritual nature and needs of men. It is the only guide of life which really leads the spirit in the way of peace and salvation. America was born a Christian nation. America was born to exemplify that devotion to the elements of righteousness which are derived from the revelations of Holy Scripture.

Woodrow Wilson | 28th president

Inside the Bible's pages lie all the answers to all the problems man has ever known. . . . It is my firm belief that the enduring values presented in its pages have a great meaning for each of us and for our nation. The Bible can touch our hearts, order our minds, and refresh our souls.

Ronald Reagan | 40th president

Hold fast to the Bible as the sheet anchor of your liberties. Write its precepts in your hearts, and practice them in your lives. To the influence of this book are we indebted for all the progress made in true civilization, and to this we must look as our guide in the future. Righteousness exalteth a nation, but sin is a reproach to any people.

ULYSSES S. GRANT | 18TH PRESIDENT

The strength of our country is the strength of its religious convictions. . . . The foundations of our society and our government rest so much on the teachings of the Bible that it would be difficult to support them if faith in these teachings would cease to be practically universal in our country.

CALVIN COOLIDGE | 30TH PRESIDENT

We cannot read the history of our rise and development as a Nation without reckoning with the place the Bible has occupied in shaping the advances of the Republic. . . . Where we have been the truest and most consistent in obeying its precepts, we have attained the greatest measure of contentment and prosperity.

FRANKLIN ROOSEVELT | 32TH PRESIDENT

DAY 3

Father,

The worries of each day are ever around us. Conflict, both within and without, threatens the peace we so desperately want and seek. Father, we come to You with open hearts, seeking Your guidance and being content with all that You have given us as a nation. Guard our hearts, O Lord, so that we will be faithful to You, and let the peace of Your presence surround us each and every day.

Be anxious for nothing, but in everything by prayer and supplication, with thanksgiving, let your requests be made known to God; and the peace of God, which surpasses all understanding, will guard your hearts and minds through Christ Jesus.

PHILIPPIANS 4:6–7

Grace, mercy, and peace will be with you from God the Father and from the Lord Jesus Christ, the Son of the Father, in truth and love.

2 JOHN 1:3

God, the Father of this nation, has promised us grace, mercy, and peace in the midst of pain and loss, sin and sorrow, worries and weariness. We can all find reasons to be concerned about our nation and the direction we're headed. Rather than being anxious, may we choose to be prayerful. Let us keep our eyes on our Sovereign Lord who has protected and sustained our nation to this point. Let us also be responsible citizens, asking God to grant us wisdom about election issues and candidates—and then casting our vote. Let us boldly exercise our freedom of choice as we seek to elect new leaders this year.

DAY 4

Father,

Humble our hearts today so that we will hear Your voice. Help us as a nation to obey Your voice in all that we say and do. Continue to bless us, O Lord, and give us a compassionate and giving heart toward those around us. Hold us to a higher calling, that we will carefully observe Your commandments and be a "nation under God with liberty and justice for all."

Now it shall come to pass, if you diligently obey the voice of the Lord your God, to observe carefully all His commandments which I command you today, that the Lord your God will set you high above all nations of the earth. And all these blessings shall come upon you and overtake you, because you obey the voice of the Lord your God: Blessed shall you be in the city, and blessed shall you be in the country.

DEUTERONOMY 28:1–3

Through your seed [Christ] all the nations of the earth shall be blessed, because you have heard and obeyed My voice.

GENESIS 22:18 AMP

God is calling this nation to obey His voice and follow His leadership. Charles Stanley said, "Obey God and leave the consequences up to Him."* We as a nation need to repent of our independence from God and choose instead to follow Him, to obey His commandments, and to turn to Him for guidance when we face decisions. He has been faithful to this nation despite our faithlessness. May our faithlessness change to faith: may we, like our founders, stand boldly in our Christian faith and truly depend on God.

---

*Charles F. Stanley, *Life Principles Bible* (Nashville: Thomas Nelson, Inc., 2009), 88.

DAY 5

Father,

We know that Your heart's desire for us is to be at peace with You and with those around us. Place within our hearts the desire to live for You and to listen to the leading of Your Spirit. Let us diligently search for You. Open our eyes that we might see what is good, honorable, and just for this country and for the well-being of all people.

I know the thoughts that I think toward you, says the
Lord, thoughts of peace and not of evil, to give you a
future and a hope. Then you will call upon Me and go
and pray to Me, and I will listen to you. And you will seek
Me and find Me, when you search for Me with all your
heart.

JEREMIAH 29:11–13

I love those who love me,
And those who seek me diligently will find me.

PROVERBS 8:17

God is not hiding from us. He is ever present with us, and He longs for each of us to know Him—not just know about Him—and to be filled with His love. That happens when we approach God with an open heart and the desire to be in a close relationship with Him. Therefore, call to Him, draw near to Him, and let each day be filled with His presence in your life. He is waiting to bless you and to bless this nation. May we live each day mindful of His presence with us, receiving the love He promises to those who love Him, and, therefore, being a light of love and hope in this dark nation.

George Washington

O eternal and everlasting God, . . . increase my faith in the sweet promises of the gospel; give me repentance from dead works; pardon my wanderings, and direct my thoughts unto thyself, the God of my salvation; Teach me how to live in thy fear, labor in thy service, and ever to run in the ways of thy commandments; Make me always watchful over my heart, that neither the terrors of conscience, the loathing of holy duties, the love of sin, nor an unwillingness to depart this life, may cast me into a spiritual slumber, But daily frame me more and more into the likeness of thy son Jesus Christ, that living in thy fear, and dying in thy favor, I may in thy appointed time attain the resurrection of the just unto eternal life bless my family, friends, and kindred.

—Undated Prayer from Washington's
Prayer Journal, Mount Vernon

DAY 6

Lord,

You have commanded us to make disciples of all nations—may we begin within our own hearts! You are the way, the truth, and the life, and we thank You for Your promise to be with us always. Give us sincerity of heart and unfailing courage to spread this good news, whether with our neighbors across the street or with lost souls across the earth. We trust in You to work through us—without You we can do nothing!

"Go therefore and make disciples of all the nations, baptizing them in the name of the Father and of the Son and of the Holy Spirit, teaching them to observe all things that I have commanded you; and lo, I am with you always, even to the end of the age."

MATTHEW 28:19–20

The LORD is my helper;
I will not fear.
What can man do to me?

HEBREWS 13:6

The Bible is very specific about how God expects us to live. The Word clearly says, "The LORD is my helper." But do we as individuals live that way? We as a nation don't turn to God for His help. May we learn to rise up and live in full dependence on Him—as our forefathers did—for when enough of us do, this nation will turn to and rely on the Helper as well.

DAY 7

Lord,

We as a people have become self-absorbed and busy with activities that bring temporal value. Help us turn our hearts back to You and Your Word so our nation will bear the fruit of righteousness and be set above all other nations! Strengthen us with the power of Your Spirit in our inner being as we strive to abide in You and to continue in faith that You will do more for us than we could ever imagine.

"If you abide in Me, and My words abide in you, you will ask what you desire, and it shall be done for you. By this My Father is glorified, that you bear much fruit; so you will be My disciples."

JOHN 15:7–8

"I am the vine, you are the branches. He who abides in Me, and I in him, bears much fruit; for without Me you can do nothing. . . . As the Father loved Me, I also have loved you; abide in My love. If you keep My commandments, you will abide in My love, just as I have kept My Father's commandments and abide in His love."

JOHN 15:5, 9–10

The Bible makes it clear: we will bear much fruit if we acknowledge that God is in charge and commit to abide in His presence. When we surrender our lives to God's love, mercy, and grace, He can use us for His good purposes. Abraham Lincoln said at the end of the Civil War, "This nation will have a new birth of freedom of the people, by the people, and for the people." Even today God can give our country a new birth of civil freedom and, more importantly, spiritual freedom.

★ ★ ★ ★

The Connection Between Religion and Democracy

Excerpt from Franklin D. Roosevelt's State of the Union to Congress in 1939

Storms from abroad directly challenge three institutions indispensable to Americans, now as always. The first is religion. It is the source of the other two—democracy and international good faith.

Religion, by teaching man his relationship to God, gives the individual a sense of his own dignity and teaches him to respect himself by respecting his neighbors.

Democracy, the practice of self-government, is a covenant among free men to respect the rights and liberties of their fellows.

International good faith, a sister of democracy, springs from the will of civilized nations of men to respect the rights and liberties of other nations of men.

In a modern civilization, all three—religion,

democracy, and international good faith—complement and support each other.

Where freedom of religion has been attacked, the attack has come from sources opposed to democracy. Where democracy has been overthrown, the spirit of free worship has disappeared. And where religion and democracy have vanished, good faith and reason in international affairs have given way to strident ambition and brute force.

An ordering of society which relegates religion, democracy, and good faith among nations to the background can find no place within it for the ideals of the Prince of Peace. The United States rejects such an ordering and retains its ancient faith.

There comes a time in the affairs of men when they must prepare to defend, not their homes alone, but the tenets of faith and humanity on which their churches, their governments, and their very civilization are founded. The defense of religion, of democracy, and of good faith among nations is all the same fight. To save one we must now make up our minds to save all.

DAY 8

Father,

Give us Your guidance and strength as we honestly confess our sins to You and to one another. And give us compassionate hearts as we pray for each other and our leaders across the country and the world. Rid us of judgment, condemnation, and pride, and fill us with a spirit of grace, mercy, and love. Create in our hearts a fervent desire to pray every day for Your leadership to reign in our lives.

Confess your trespasses to one another, and pray for one another, that you may be healed. The effective, fervent prayer of a righteous man avails much.

JAMES 5:16

If we confess our sins, He is faithful and just to forgive us our sins and to cleanse us from all unrighteousness.

1 JOHN 1:9

We, in this country, are not perfect. We often disappoint our Father God with the ways we conduct ourselves and the way we treat others. Thankfully, God has promised to forgive us when we confess our sins both individually and, corporately, as Americans. What a blessing! What a privilege! Let us daily seek God's direction and boldly go before the throne of grace for ourselves and on behalf of our nation and its leaders. God is waiting with open arms.

DAY 9

Father,

Your Word says that if we delight ourselves in You, You will give us the desires of our hearts (Psalm 37:4). Please direct our paths in Your ways everlasting so that Your will becomes our desire, so that Your way becomes our delight. Fill us with the power of Your presence and bind us together as a people of one nation under God. And through each day, to You be the glory for all goodness and blessings that come our way.

The sacrifice of the wicked is an abomination to
        the LORD,
But the prayer of the upright is His delight.

PROVERBS 15:8

He [whom God has saved from the Pit] shall
pray to God, and He will delight in him,
He shall see His face with joy,
For He restores to man His righteousness.

JOB 33:26

T he power of prayer is evident throughout the Bible. The effect it has on us
individually and the impact it can have on
nations are profound. Whenever we open our
hearts to God, He hears our prayers and gives
us direction. So may we as a nation come
together in prayer, humbly walk in God's
ways, and earnestly seek His guidance. Then
we will know His delight, find joy in His presence, and receive His favor.

DAY 10

Father,

The joy of the Lord is our strength; therefore, let us rejoice as a nation and as a people that have been blessed beyond all that we could ask or conceive. Let us pray each day for Your divine guidance, O Lord, and never forget Your benefits. Thank You, Lord, that You welcome us to Your throne of grace to receive Your blessing.

Rejoice always, pray without ceasing, in everything give thanks; for this is the will of God in Christ Jesus for you.

1 THESSALONIANS 5:16–18

Oh, give thanks to the LORD, for He is good!
For His mercy endures forever.

1 CHRONICLES 16:34

Throughout the Bible God continually calls us to give thanks, and because of His goodness, we always have reason to do exactly that. Consider too the reasons we can give thanks: we have freedom, privileges, and blessings that people in other parts of the world would struggle to imagine. It is absolutely fitting that we give thanks to the Lord for our country even as we pray for its future. May we faithfully pray each day for wisdom and discernment for every American as we prepare to vote in November.

For Our Country

Almighty God, who has given us this good land for our heritage, we humbly beseech Thee that we may always prove ourselves a people mindful of Thy favor and glad to do Thy will. Bless our land with honorable ministry, sound learning, and pure manners. Save us from violence, discord, and confusion, from pride and arrogance, and from every evil way. Defend our liberties, and fashion into one united people the multitude brought hither out of many kindreds and tongues. Endow with Thy spirit of wisdom those to whom in Thy name we entrust the authority of government, that there may be justice and peace at home, and that through obedience to Thy law, we may show forth Thy praise among the nations of the earth. In time of prosperity fill our hearts with thankfulness, and in the day of trouble, suffer not our trust in Thee to fail; all of which we ask through Jesus Christ our Lord. Amen.

—1928 United States
Book of Common Prayer

DAY 11

Thank You, Lord, for the gift of Your Spirit, who continually helps us overcome our weaknesses. We confess that all things are possible through You and nothing is possible without You! Open our hearts and intercede with the Father that we may humble ourselves in Your presence. We thank You for Your forgiveness. Strengthen us to live with purpose and empower us to serve You.

The Spirit also helps in our weaknesses. For we do not know what we should pray for as we ought, but the Spirit Himself makes intercession for us with groanings which cannot be uttered.

ROMANS 8:26

Now He who searches the hearts knows what the mind of the Spirit is, because He makes intercession for the saints according to the will of God. And we know that all things work together for good to those who love God, to those who are the called according to His purpose.

ROMANS 8:27–28

We who name Jesus as Lord are blessed to have the gift of His Holy Spirit. Each day we can rely on the Spirit for direction, wisdom, reassurance, and peace in our daily lives. The Spirit is also a tireless Intercessor for when we are tired, empty, or unsure about how to pray for our darkened nation and hurting world. And it is the Spirit who will enable us to help this nation be a beacon for Christ, which is our calling. Let us live each day to make a difference in the direction our country is moving.

DAY 12

Lord,

You are the Rock and Strength of this nation. You are the only One who can deliver us from our enemies. We trust in You and pray humbly for Your guidance and direction for this great nation. Give us wisdom to make right choices. Help us live in such a way that Your name will be honored in all things. May You forever be praised.

The LORD is my rock and my fortress and my deliverer;
My God, my strength, in whom I will trust;
My shield and the horn of my salvation, my stronghold.
I will call upon the LORD, who is worthy to be praised;
So shall I be saved from my enemies.

PSALM 18:2–3

The Lord is my strength and song,
And He has become my salvation;
He is my God, and I will praise Him;
My father's God, and I will exalt Him.

EXODUS 15:2

If and when our nation fully turns to God, He will provide for us strength, wisdom, and purpose. He will bless us even as we deal with the consequences of our sinful straying, and He will bless us by redeeming some of our many missteps. Each day we should praise Him and thank Him for His faithfulness, His grace, and for His ability to make all things new. May we as a nation daily seek Him and His direction for our good and His glory. "God is my strength and power, and He makes my way perfect" (2 Samuel 22:33).

DAY 13

Father,

We exalt our praise and adoration to You all throughout the day and night! May we never forget that You are merciful and gracious, and that You, our Creator, receive our devotion and prayers with an attentive, listening ear. Give us eyes to see the splendor of Your holiness and ears to hear the majesty of Your voice as You lead us to holy and righteous living.

Evening and morning and at noon
I will pray, and cry aloud,
And He shall hear my voice.

PSALM 55:17

My voice You shall hear in the morning,
*   O LORD;*
In the morning I will direct it to You,
And I will look up.

PSALM 5:3

Every day, throughout each day, we have an open invitation from God to go to Him in prayer. And our heavenly Father has promised to hear our prayers. In light of that promise, we would be wise to earnestly seek God's direction on a daily basis. God has made it very clear that He will hear our prayers of confession on behalf of our country, as well as prayers for His direction for our lives. Choosing to pray brings great benefits that we as a nation desperately need.

The Reason Why We Vote

The time has come that Christians must vote for honest men, and take consistent ground in politics. . . . God cannot sustain this free and blessed country, which we love and pray for, unless the Church will take right ground. . . . It seems sometimes as if the foundations of the nation are becoming rotten, and Christians seem to act as if they think God does not see what they do in politics.

CHARLES FINNEY

If America is to survive, we must elect more God-centered men and women to public office—individuals who will seek Divine guidance in the affairs of state.

BILLY GRAHAM

God commands you to choose for rulers just men who will rule in the fear of God. The preservation of a republican government depends on the faithful discharge of this duty; if the citizens neglect their duty and place unprincipled men in office, the government will soon be corrupted; laws will be made, not for the public good, so much as for selfish or local purposes; corrupt or incompetent men will be appointed to execute the laws; the public revenues will be squandered on unworthy men; and the rights of the citizens will be violated or disregarded.

NOAH WEBSTER
Born 1758 - Died 1843
"The Schoolmaster of the Republic."

NOAH WEBSTER

The liberties of our Country, the freedom of our civil constitution, are worth defending at all hazards; and it is our duty to defend them against all attacks. We have received them as a fair Inheritance from our worthy Ancestors: they purchased them for us with toil and danger and expense of treasure and blood, and transmitted them to us with care and diligence. It will bring an everlasting mark of infamy on the present generation, enlightened as it is, if we should suffer them to be wrested from us by violence without a struggle or to be cheated out of them by the artifices of false and designing men.

SAMUEL ADAMS

41

DAY 14

Father,

We humbly come before You and ask that Your Spirit reach across the lands to all who are hurting and spiritually lost. Restore their hearts with hope everlasting; comfort them with Your tender, loving arms. May we be sensitive to their needs, whether physical or spiritual, and be eager and willing to share Your love for them, just as You have bestowed Your love upon us.

We give thanks to the God and Father of our Lord Jesus Christ, praying always for you, since we heard of your faith in Christ Jesus and of your love for all the saints.

COLOSSIANS 1:3–4

Oh, give thanks to the LORD, for He is good!
  For His mercy endures forever.
Oh, give thanks to the God of gods!
  For His mercy endures forever.
Oh, give thanks to the Lord of lords!
  For His mercy endures forever.

PSALM 136:1–3

I don't think we could adequately thank the Lord for the work our forefathers did to establish this nation on Christian principles and with protection for the freedom to worship God. We are still blessed today to be able to worship God and to thank Him for this and many other freedoms. May we willingly and boldly defend the precious rights we enjoy, the rights to attend the church of our choice and to elect the leaders of our country.

DAY 15

Father,

May Your love flow through and around us. Speak to our hearts and open our minds that we may see You and the light of Your glory. Cleanse us, O Lord, that we may stand before You without blemish. Help us as a nation to be a discerning people with moral voices who will bring honor and glory to You, O God.

This I pray, that your love may abound still more and more in knowledge and all discernment, that you may approve the things that are excellent, that you may be sincere and without offense till the day of Christ.

PHILIPPIANS 1:9–10

May the Lord make you increase and abound
in love to one another and to all, just as we do
to you, so that He may establish your hearts
blameless in holiness before our God and Father
at the coming of our Lord Jesus Christ with all
His saints.

1 THESSALONIANS 3:12–13

Brotherly love in America has long helped hold this country together. Throughout our history, we have also cared for the human rights and basic needs of individuals around the world. There is no greater gift to humankind than to love our neighbors as ourselves and to care for those less fortunate. May God continue to place in our hearts a deep, abiding love for one another, our American neighbors as well as our international ones.

ABRAHAM LINCOLN

F ondly do we hope—fervently do we pray—that this mighty scourge of war may speedily pass away. Yet, if God wills that it continue . . . until every drop of blood drawn with the lash shall be paid by another drawn with the sword . . . so still it must be said "the judgments of the Lord are true and righteous altogether."

With malice toward none, with charity for all, with firmness in the right, as God gives us to see the right, let us strive on to finish the work we are in, to bind up the nation's wounds, to care for him who shall have borne the battle and for his widow and for his orphans—to do all which may achieve and cherish a just and a lasting peace among ourselves and with all nations.

—SECOND INAUGURAL ADDRESS, MARCH 4, 1865

DAY 16

Lord,

We bow before You in humble thanksgiving for Your gifts of power and strength, fortitude and might! We claim the riches of Your glory and the fullness of Your grace that come through the indwelling of Your Spirit within us. We pray for our nation to remain firm and steadfast in the knowledge of Your truth and the promise of the victory that is ours through Christ, who loves us.

I bow my knees to the Father of our Lord Jesus Christ, from whom the whole family in heaven and earth is named, that He would grant you, according to the riches of His glory, to be strengthened with might through His Spirit in the inner man . . . to know the love of Christ which passes knowledge; that you may be filled with all the fullness of God.

EPHESIANS 3:14–16, 19

[I pray for fellow believers] that their hearts may be encouraged, being knit together in love, and attaining to all riches of the full assurance of understanding, to the knowledge of the mystery of God, both of the Father and of Christ, in whom are hidden all the treasures of wisdom and knowledge.

COLOSSIANS 2:2–3

When we stand together as a nation united under God, willing to defend the rights that have been given to us, we will be blessed. The freedom we so enjoy comes with the responsibility—of every citizen—to defend that freedom. God can also use His people in this land to share His love and offer encouragement to neighbors. May His Spirit be our Guide as we go forward as His people and as Americans who need to guard our land.

DAY 17

O Lord,

We lift our voices and praise Your holy name! May
You forever be the center of our thoughts, that in
all things we may lift You up in worship and song.
Let the words of our mouths and the meditations of
our hearts be a sweet aroma to You, for You are our
King—our joy comes from You! Righteousness and
justice are the foundation of Your throne; therefore,
we praise Your holy name forever.

I will sing to the LORD as long as I live;
I will sing praise to my God while I have my being.
May my meditation be sweet to Him;
I will be glad in the LORD.

PSALM 104:33–34

*I will praise the L*ORD *according to His*
righteousness,
*And will sing praise to the name of the L*ORD
Most High.

PSALM 7:17

Praising God should be an everyday and throughout-the-day occurrence in this great country we call home. We are blessed with the freedom to live as we wish, vote as we choose, worship where we want to, and express our opinion without fear of retribution. These are privileges we should not take for granted. May God be our guide this November as we plan for the future and prayerfully exercise our right to vote.

DAY 18

O Lord,

We beg You to hear our supplications. Do not let our words fall on deaf ears. Let us come to You each morning with hearts full of joy, for You are our Most High God, and everything we have comes from You. Bless us that we might bless others. Let us always look to You for every provision. Let us each be an open vessel filled with Your wisdom, that others might know Your saving grace.

Give ear to my words, O Lord,
Consider my meditation.
Give heed to the voice of my cry,
My King and my God,
For to You I will pray.
My voice You shall hear in the morning, O Lord;
In the morning I will direct it to You,
And I will look up.

PSALM 5:1–3

"When you pray, go into your room, and when you have shut your door, pray to your Father who is in the secret place; and your Father who sees in secret will reward you openly."

MATTHEW 6:6

Time and again, the Bible urges us to go to God in prayer and reminds us that He has promised to listen to our prayers and answer them. Since our nation's very first days, God's work in this country has been both invited and sustained by the prayers of His people. Throughout history the persistent, prevailing, intentional, and never-ending prayers of God's people have made a difference in this nation, a difference that we won't fully know this side of heaven.

The Gettysburg Address

—ABRAHAM LINCOLN

F our score and seven years ago our fathers brought forth on this continent a new nation, conceived in Liberty, and dedicated to the proposition that all men are created equal.

Now we are engaged in a great civil war, testing whether that nation, or any nation so conceived and so dedicated, can long endure. We are met on a great battlefield of that war. We have come to dedicate a portion of that field, as a final resting place for those who here gave their lives that that nation might live. It is altogether fitting and proper that we should do this.

But, in a larger sense, we cannot dedicate—we cannot consecrate—we cannot hallow this ground. The brave men, living and dead, who struggled here, have consecrated it, far above our poor power to add or detract. The world will little note, nor long remember what we say here, but it can never forget what they did here. It is for us the living, rather, to be dedicated here to the unfinished work which they who fought here have thus far so nobly advanced. It is rather for us to be here dedicated to the great task remaining before us—that from these honored dead we take increased devotion to that cause for which they gave the last full measure of devotion—that we here highly resolve that these dead shall not have died in vain—that this nation, under God, shall have a new birth of freedom—and that government of the people, by the people, for the people, shall not perish from the earth.

DAY 19

Father,

You are so wonderful! Through Jesus Christ we have an open invitation to come to You in prayer. We give thanks for this blessing and each day find joy in all that You give to us. What a blessed people we are to know and embrace Your unconditional love.

Hear me when I call, O God of my righteousness!
You have relieved me in my distress;
Have mercy on me, and hear my prayer.

PSALM 4:1

All the paths of the LORD are mercy and truth,
To such as keep His covenant and His
testimonies.

PSALM 25:10

Throughout the Bible the Lord's people cry out for His mercy. Today we also greatly need mercy from our heavenly Father. God's mercy—like His grace and love—is available to all of us who humble ourselves before Him and turn our hearts toward Him. We as a nation will not survive without God's direction and His gracious redemption. He has promised to listen when we go to Him in prayer. So let us pray that God prompts His people to vote, guides those votes, and then gives the elected leaders the wisdom they need to lead this great nation on the right path in the days ahead.

DAY 20

Father,

We thank You for hearing our petition. Strengthen us by the power of Your Spirit to live in such a way that glorifies You. Forgive us when we do things that displease You and separate us from Your presence. Lead us each day, that we might live lives that are pleasing to You. May You forever be praised.

The Lord has heard my supplication;
The Lord will receive my prayer.

PSALM 6:9

"Ask, and it will be given to you; seek, and you will find; knock, and it will be opened to you. For everyone who asks receives, and he who seeks finds, and to him who knocks it will be opened."

LUKE 11:9–10

God has extended to us an open invitation to go to Him in prayer, and He has promised that when we knock, the door will be opened. But we must persevere in our prayers. We are to keep knocking, we are to pray daily and throughout each day, and when answers are slow to come, we are to continue laying our heartfelt requests before Him. He has promised to provide wisdom and direction when we seek His good and perfect will for us and for our nation.

FRANKLIN D. ROOSEVELT

Almighty God: Our sons, pride of our Nation, this day have set upon a mighty endeavor, a struggle to preserve our Republic, our religion, and our civilization, and to set free a suffering humanity. . . .

Lead them straight and true; give strength to their arms, stoutness to their hearts, steadfastness in their faith. . . .

Their road will be long and hard. For the enemy is strong. . . . Success may not come with rushing speed, but we shall return again and again; and we know that by Thy grace, and by the righteousness of our cause, our sons will triumph. . . .

With Thy blessing, we shall prevail over the unholy forces of our enemy. Help us to conquer the apostles of greed and racial arrogancies. Lead us to the saving of our country, and with our sister Nations into a world unity that will spell a sure peace, a peace invulnerable to the schemings of unworthy men. And a peace that will let all of men live in freedom, reaping the just rewards of their honest toil.

—D-DAY, JUNE 6, 1944

DAY 21

Father,

We praise You for Your grace, mercy, and loving-kindness. May we as a nation look to You with thanksgiving in our hearts for the blessings You have poured upon us. Let us forever rest in the shadow of Your wings and shout for joy with praise, for You are a most gracious God, and You bless us even beyond our understanding.

Because Your lovingkindness is better than life,
My lips shall praise You.
Thus I will bless You while I live;
I will lift up my hands in Your name. . . .
Because You have been my help,
Therefore in the shadow of Your wings I will rejoice.

PSALM 63:3–4, 7

I will bless the LORD at all times;
His praise shall continually be in my mouth.
My soul shall make its boast in the LORD;
The humble shall hear of it and be glad.
Oh, magnify the LORD with me,
And let us exalt His name together.

PSALM 34:1–3

The psalmist modeled what God desires from us. He was committed to blessing the Lord at all times, to praising Him continually, and to telling others of His great love for all of humanity. When we magnify the Lord and lift Him up, we find ourselves blessed by a more real sense of His presence with us and a genuine joy in His love for us. Imagine a nation united in seeking to magnify the Lord, a nation committed to blessing the Lord in word and deed. What a blessed people they would be! What a blessed people we would be. Let us seek God with fervency and confidence.

DAY 22

Father,

We recognize that there are those who would speak evil against You when hardship knocks at their door. Let us forever stand firm in the foundation of our faith. Let us live in the center of Your will. We will come to You each day for strength and endurance. Help us, O God, to be the people You wish us to be, for we trust in You.

Hear my cry, O God;
Attend to my prayer.
From the end of the earth I will cry to You,
When my heart is overwhelmed;
Lead me to the rock that is higher than I.
For You have been a shelter for me,
A strong tower from the enemy.
I will abide in Your tabernacle forever;
I will trust in the shelter of Your wings.

PSALM 61:1–4

I have set the LORD always before me;
Because He is at my right hand I shall not
be moved.

PSALM 16:8

The Bible clearly tells us that our strength comes from the Lord: "For the eyes of the LORD run to and fro throughout the whole earth, to give strong support to those whose heart is blameless toward him" (2 Chronicles 16:9 ESV). May we look to the Lord with all our hearts for strength and courage to stand up for biblical truth and Christian morals. God has promised that He will always be with us and will always go before us. Therefore, let us stand firm in our faith, trusting that our powerful God has this nation in His hands and choosing to believe that one day the Christian principles in which we believe shall guide this nation.

DAY 23

Lord,

We are so blessed that each day You come to us with the gift of Your Spirit to help us and strengthen our purpose for Your glory. Continue to work in us, O Lord, and help us grow to be the people You wish us to be. Thank You for Your continued goodness even when we stumble; thank You that You are ever present to hold our hands and lift us up. Your unconditional love has been promised forever. Thank You for Your gracious mercy to us each day.

You, O my God, have revealed to Your servant that You will build him a house. Therefore Your servant has found it in his heart to pray before You. And now, LORD, You are God, and have promised this goodness to Your servant. Now You have been pleased to bless the house of Your servant, that it may continue before You forever; for You have blessed it, O LORD, and it shall be blessed forever.

1 CHRONICLES 17:25–27

Blessed is the man You choose,
And cause to approach You,
That he may dwell in Your courts.
We shall be satisfied with the goodness of
          Your house,
Of Your holy temple.

PSALM 65:4

God has blessed this nation with economic and material prosperity. He allowed us to become the most powerful country in the world and, through the years, enabled us to overcome staggering obstacles. God has placed His hand upon us and has been pleased to bless us as we honor Him. Let us never forget or stop thanking God for the bountiful blessings that He has so graciously and generously bestowed on us.

"I Have a Dream"

—Martin Luther King Jr.

Now is the time to rise from the dark and desolate valley of segregation to the sunlit path of racial justice.... Now is the time to make justice a reality for all of God's children....

I have a dream that one day this nation will rise up and live out the true meaning of its creed: "We hold these truths to be self-evident: that all men are created equal."

I have a dream that one day on the red hills of Georgia, the sons of former slaves and the sons of former slave owners will be able to sit down together at the table of brotherhood....

I have a dream that my four little children will one day live in a nation where they will not be judged by the color of their skin but by the content of their character....

This is our hope. This is the faith that I go back to the South with.

With this faith, we will be able to hew out of the mountain of despair a stone of hope. With this faith, we will be able to transform the jangling discords of our nation into a beautiful symphony of brotherhood. With this faith, we will be able to work together, to pray together, to struggle together, to go to jail together, to stand up for freedom together, knowing that we will be free one day. . . .

From every mountainside, let freedom ring. And when this happens, when we allow freedom to ring, when we let it ring from every village and every hamlet, from every state and every city, we will be able to speed up that day when all of God's children, black men and white men, Jews and Gentiles, Protestants and Catholics, will be able to join hands and sing in the words of the old Negro spiritual, "Free at last! Free at last! Thank God Almighty, we are free at last!"

DAY 24

Father,

Help our nation with its unbelief! Lead us into a renewed relationship with You! Forgive us when we find fault in our brothers. Help us look beyond their shortcomings and look deeper within ourselves to become better people. Forgive us when we fall short of doing all that You've called us to do, and when we fail to demonstrate love and forgiveness toward those who wrong us. Thank You for the blessing of knowing that we are forgiven—no matter what.

"Whatever things you ask when you pray, believe that you receive them, and you will have them. And whenever you stand praying, if you have anything against anyone, forgive him, that your Father in heaven may also forgive you your trespasses."

MARK 11:24–25

O Lord, hear! O Lord, forgive! O Lord, listen and act! Do not delay for Your own sake, my God, for Your city and Your people are called by Your name.

DANIEL 9:19

We are not perfect people; every human being throughout time has, does, and will need forgiveness—from God but also from one another. If we are to come together as a nation with one voice and one purpose, we must learn to forgive each other as God has forgiven us. Unity means strength, so may nothing cause disunity and weakness. May we as believers seek to be all that God has called us to be. May we as a nation seek to be all that we are privileged to be.

DAY 25

Lord,

We come to You with open hearts and ask that You speak to our spirits with words of wisdom and direction, that we may know how You wish for us to pray. Help Your humble servants to speak words of praise and adoration, for You are the King of kings and the Lord of lords. Teach us, Lord, that we may know You and the power of Your resurrection. Fill us with Your presence and forgive our shortcomings. Lead us, O Lord, to a higher place, that You might be lifted up and draw all men to You.

Now it came to pass, as [Jesus] was praying in a certain place, when He ceased, that one of His disciples said to Him, "Lord, teach us to pray, as John also taught his disciples."

LUKE 11:1

[A repentant man] shall pray to God, and He
will delight in him,
He shall see His face with joy,
For He restores to man His righteousness.

JOB 33:26

From the beginning of this remarkable nation, in both good times and hard times, prayer has been a key component in every gathering of Congress and presidents. God has provided a unique opportunity for each and every one of us—and us collectively as a nation—to go to Him with confession, praise, thanksgiving, and supplication. The Lord has promised to listen to those prayers, to respond, to reassure, and to enable us to glorify Him however He chooses to answer.

JOHN F. KENNEDY

L et us therefore proclaim our gratitude to Providence for manifold blessings—let us be humbly thankful for inherited ideals—and let us resolve to share those blessings and those ideals with our fellow human beings throughout the world. . . .

On that day let us gather in sanctuaries dedicated to worship and in homes blessed by family affection to express our gratitude for the glorious gifts of God; and let us earnestly and humbly pray that He will continue to guide and sustain us in the great unfinished tasks of achieving peace, justice, and understanding among all men and nations and of ending misery and suffering wherever they exist.

—WRITTEN FOR THANKSGIVING DAY 1963

DAY 26

Lord,

There are so many times when we have burdens almost too heavy to bear. Our nation faces hardships and pain; we need Your wisdom and help in all areas. Strengthen us as a people and lead us in the way that will bring honor and glory to You. Lord, You have promised that if we humble ourselves and seek Your face and pray, You will heal our land. May we forever be humble in Your sight, and may we experience Your blessings in the midst of our great need.

Give ear to my prayer, O God,
And do not hide Yourself from my supplication.
Attend to me, and hear me;
I am restless in my complaint, and moan noisily.

PSALM 55:1–2

Let us therefore come boldly to the throne of grace, that we may obtain mercy and find grace to help in time of need.

HEBREWS 4:16

In times of crisis, this country has always gone boldly before the throne of God seeking His divine mercy and grace. Each time God has responded to our prayers with grace, mercy, and love. Today we face significant decisions, if not borderline crises. Will we, as a Christian nation, stand strong together with the one purpose of honoring God in all that we say and do? We can only be one nation under God if He is our guiding light. May nothing keep us from walking in step with the One who is the Author of history, the God who guides, judges, and blesses.

DAY 27

Father,

You are so wonderful. Thank You for caring about our burdens. Open our hearts to Your Spirit and let us listen to Your voice. Strengthen us, O God, with confidence in You, that we may live for You and glorify Your name. Father, we praise You for all the gifts that You have given us. Draw us close to You that we may see Your glory.

Cast your burden on the LORD,
And He shall sustain you;
He shall never permit the righteous to be moved.

PSALM 55:22

Brethren, if a man is overtaken in any trespass, you who are spiritual restore such a one in a spirit of gentleness, considering yourself lest you also be tempted. Bear one another's burdens, and so fulfill the law of Christ.

GALATIANS 6:1–2

The Founding Fathers came together, unified in their work, toward one goal and one purpose: to establish a government that allowed freedom and justice to reign. Two important freedoms were those of speech and of worship, and for more than two hundred years we have enjoyed these gifts our forefathers established as foundational to life in these United States. May we Americans continue to stand together, bearing one another's burdens, protecting our freedoms, and praying for this land.

DAY 28

Father,

True wisdom is a gift that only You, Father, can give. May we always be in right standing with You. Let the words we speak honor You, and let us never speak Your name in vain. Let us stay steadfast and live in such a way that Your light will shine through us wherever we go. Thank You, Father, for Your mercy and love.

The mouth of the righteous speaks wisdom,
And his tongue talks of justice.
The law of his God is in his heart;
None of his steps shall slide.

PSALM 37:30–31

Lead me, O Lord, in Your righteousness because
of my enemies;
Make Your way straight before my face. . . .
For You, O Lord, will bless the righteous;
With favor You will surround him as with a shield.

PSALM 5:8, 12

We have been given the privilege and responsibility of representing the love of God and sharing His truth with all the world. May we not neglect doing so in our own nation. We need God to enable us to lead a winsome life that reveals the love of Jesus Christ and compels people to want to know Him. This kind of life begins when we are in fellowship with God. He has promised to bless the righteous with His favor and surround us with a shield; therefore, let us allow nothing to interfere with our commitment to live as a Christian nation that honors God in all that we say and do.

The Four Freedoms

—President Franklin D. Roosevelt

January 1941

No realistic American can expect from a dictator's peace international generosity, or return of true independence, or world disarmament, or freedom of expression, or freedom of religion—or even good business.

Such a peace would bring no security for us or for our neighbors. "Those who would give up essential liberty to purchase a little temporary safety, deserve neither liberty nor safety." . . .

In the future days, which we seek to make secure, we look forward to a world founded upon four essential human freedoms.

The first is freedom of speech and expression—everywhere in the world.

The second is freedom of every person to worship God in his own way—everywhere in the world.

The third is freedom from want—which, translated into world terms, means economic understandings which will secure to every nation a healthy peacetime life for its inhabitants—everywhere in the world.

The fourth is freedom from fear—which, translated into world terms, means a worldwide reduction of armaments to such a point and in such a thorough fashion that no nation will be in a position to commit an act of physical aggression against any neighbor—anywhere in the world.

That is no vision of a distant millennium. It is a definite basis for a kind of world attainable in our own time and generation. That kind of world is the very antithesis of the so-called new order of tyranny which the dictators seek to create with the crash of a bomb. . . .

This nation has placed its destiny in the hands and heads and hearts of its millions of free men and women; and its faith in freedom under the guidance of God. Freedom means the supremacy of human rights everywhere. Our support goes to those who struggle to gain those rights or keep them. Our strength is our unity of purpose. To that high concept there can be no end save victory.

DAY 29

O Lord,

Strengthen our faith. Help us never to doubt Your Word or Your faithfulness. Lift us up that we may boldly proclaim Your truth each and every day. Let us be sensitive to the leading of Your Spirit and never forget that "I can do all things through Christ who strengthens me" (Philippians 4:13). Lord, we praise You because Your mercies are new every morning and Your faithfulness is great.

Jesus answered and said to [His disciples], "Assuredly, I say to you, if you have faith and do not doubt, you will not only do what was done to the fig tree, but also if you say to this mountain, 'Be removed and be cast into the sea,' it will be done. And whatever things you ask in prayer, believing, you will receive."

MATTHEW 21:21–22

It is good to give thanks to the LORD,
And to sing praises to Your name, O Most High;
To declare Your lovingkindness in the morning,
And Your faithfulness every night.

PSALM 92:1–2

On several occasions and with varying words, the psalmists proclaimed that God's faithfulness endures for all generations. We can absolutely count on God in every circumstance in our lives—and in the lives of our children, grandchildren, and great-grandchildren. But can He count on our faithfulness both individually and corporately? Declaring His loving-kindness to one another each day will help bind us together as a nation and encourage us to speak boldly of our faith in Jesus Christ. God will honor those actions as we demonstrate His precious love for all humanity.

DAY 30

Lord,

Our nation needs Your guidance and direction. We humbly ask that Your Spirit intercede with the leaders of the nation, giving them the wisdom to make decisions that will honor You. We pray fervently for peace both here and abroad. Let us live with reverence for You and with peace in our hearts for our fellow man. We know this is Your desire. May we always remember that You are our God and Savior.

I exhort first of all that supplications, prayers, intercession, and giving of thanks be made for all men, for kings and all who are in authority, that we may lead a quiet and peaceable life in all godliness and reverence. For this is good and acceptable in the sight of God our Savior.

1 TIMOTHY 2:1–3

Bodily exercise profits a little, but godliness is profitable for all things, having promise of the life that now is and of that which is to come. This is a faithful saying and worthy of all acceptance.

1 TIMOTHY 4:8–9

"Godliness is profitable for all things"—and godliness means simply being devoted to God. Simple, but not easy. Clearly it hasn't been and isn't easy for our nation to be devoted to God. The USA struggles to place God first in what she says and what she does. But the state of our country will not and cannot improve until God becomes the top priority in our lives. When we as a nation come together with the single purpose of lifting up Jesus Christ, God will restore our nation and bless our land. We are a great country that has been blessed with favor and prosperity for more than 230 years. Therefore, let godliness be our shining beacon.

RONALD REAGAN

To preserve our blessed land we must look to God. . . . It is time to realize that we need God more than He needs us. . . .

Let us, young and old, join together, as did the First Continental Congress, in the first step, in humble heartfelt prayer. Let us do so for the love of God and His great goodness, in search of His guidance and the grace of repentance, in seeking His blessings, His peace, and the resting of His kind and holy hands on ourselves, our nation, our friends in the defense of freedom, and all mankind, now and always.

The time has come to turn to God and reassert our trust in Him for the healing of America. . . . Our country is in need of and ready for a spiritual renewal. Today, we utter no prayer more fervently than the ancient prayer for peace on Earth.

"The Lord bless you and keep you; the Lord make His face to shine upon you and be gracious unto you; the Lord lift up His countenance upon you and give you peace. . . ." And God bless you all.

—FROM A SPEECH TO THE AMERICAN PEOPLE
FEBRUARY 6, 1986

DAY 31

O Lord,

Let us never forget to praise Your holy name. You are a wonderful God. You are slow to anger and patient, with an unconditional love that has no end. Let us bless You each day and lift up our thanks in praise for the wonderful things You have done for us. May we forever give honor to Your name, for without You we are nothing.

Because Your lovingkindness is better than life,
My lips shall praise You.
Thus I will bless You while I live;
I will lift up my hands in Your name.
My soul shall be satisfied as with marrow and fatness,
And my mouth shall praise You with joyful lips.

PSALM 63:3–5

O Lord, open my lips,
And my mouth shall show forth Your praise.

PSALM 51:15

When we make praising the Lord a habit, our lives will change. Everything we do will be different as pleasing God becomes more important and knowing more about Him becomes a priority. When we choose to live as the hands and feet of Jesus, we daily declare the love of Christ—and that can bring light and hope to our country. The more we praise God with our lives as well as our mouths, the more He comes alive in us—and that can attract others to start following Him. So may we—as the psalmist modeled—open our lips in praise to almighty God!

DAY 32

Father,

In Your Word You have given us a guide for life and have asked us to meditate on Your Word day and night. Place that desire within our hearts. Give us a sincere hunger for Your Word, that we may know You better and know more clearly how You want us to live. Keep us feeding on Your Word, that we may honor You in all we say and do.

This Book of the Law shall not depart from your mouth, but you shall meditate in it day and night, that you may observe to do according to all that is written in it. For then you will make your way prosperous, and then you will have good success.

JOSHUA 1:8

I will meditate on Your precepts,
And contemplate Your ways. . . .
Make me understand the way of Your precepts;
So shall I meditate on Your wonderful works. . . .
My eyes are awake through the night watches,
That I may meditate on Your word.

PSALM 119:15, 27, 148

Throughout the Bible, God calls His people to meditate on His law, His work, His precepts, and His Word. In His Scripture, God shows us how to live in the fellowship with Him that He desires to have with us. Our meditating on God's truth sensitizes us to His presence. We notice He is speaking to our hearts, embracing us with His love, and guiding us so that we might bring glory to His name. The more people who listen to God's voice, receive His love, and follow His guidance, the better off our nation will be.

DAY 33

Lord,

Your loving-kindness is new every day. May we forever trust in You with all our hearts and find rest in the shelter of Your love. The very life we live comes from You alone. Bless us, O Lord, with the light of Your presence, and place within us the desire to share Your light so that others may come to know the saving grace of our Lord and Savior.

How precious is Your lovingkindness, O God!
Therefore the children of men put their trust under the
          shadow of Your wings.
They are abundantly satisfied with the fullness of Your
          house,
And You give them drink from the river of Your pleasures.
For with You is the fountain of life;
In Your light we see light.

PSALM 36:7–9

He [who sat on the throne] said to me, "It is done! I am the Alpha and the Omega, the Beginning and the End. I will give of the fountain of the water of life freely to him who thirsts."

REVELATION 21:6

Jesus openly offers us the fountain of living water that springs up to everlasting life. To drink from that fountain, we must first turn away from all that separates us from God's love and then turn to Jesus, recognizing Him as our Savior and naming Him our Lord. The One who refers to Himself as the "Alpha and the Omega, the Beginning and the End" freely and without hesitation offers us living water. We drink that life-giving water as, each day, we walk hand in hand with Him. His promise is unconditional love, unshakeable joy, and peace that passes all understanding. These are ours when we say yes to God. As more of us Americans say yes to God, may our nation come to say yes to Him as well.

Psalm 119:33–40

Teach me, O Lord, the way of Your statutes,

And I shall keep it to the end.

Give me understanding, and I shall keep Your law;

Indeed, I shall observe it with my whole heart.

Make me walk in the path of Your commandments,

For I delight in it.

Incline my heart to Your testimonies,

And not to covetousness.

Turn away my eyes from looking at worthless things,

And revive me in Your way.

Establish Your word to Your servant,

Who is devoted to fearing You.

Turn away my reproach which I dread,

For Your judgments are good.

Behold, I long for Your precepts;

Revive me in Your righteousness.

DAY 34

O Lord,

Today we face many hardships in a time when our faith is continually tested. But we know there is nothing to fear because You, Lord, are in control of all things. You are our Strength and our Defender; there is nothing too hard for You. Therefore, let us be confident in our faith and bold in telling others of Your marvelous unconditional love.

The LORD is my light and my salvation;
Whom shall I fear?
The LORD is the strength of my life;
Of whom shall I be afraid?

PSALM 27:1

The LORD is my strength and my shield;
My heart trusted in Him, and I am helped;
Therefore my heart greatly rejoices,
And with my song I will praise Him.
The LORD is their strength,
And He is the saving refuge of His anointed.

PSALM 28:7–8

The Word of God tells us that the Lord is our Strength and our Shield, so we have nothing to fear. God has promised to walk beside us and go before us when we choose to live in a committed relationship with Him. Each of us faces adversity in life, but God is our Strength. In times of trouble, let us run to Him who has promised to be our Comfort and Refuge, our Redeemer and Friend. Every nation also faces adversity; may ours find God as her strength.

DAY 35

Lord,

You are the Creator of the universe—we praise Your blessed and holy name! You alone are the provider of all things, and with You all things are possible—may You always be lifted up! Let us live each day in the center of Your will and live for Your glory. If we say nothing, the rocks will cry out Your magnificent name. Let all men praise Your holy name, for You are a marvelous God, and Your light shines over all who choose to call You Lord.

I will bless the LORD at all times;
His praise shall continually be in my mouth. . . .
Oh, magnify the LORD with me,
And let us exalt His name together.

PSALM 34:1, 3

Praise the LORD, call upon His name;
Declare His deeds among the peoples,
Make mention that His name is exalted.

ISAIAH 12:4

The Bible teaches us to praise the Lord and share with others the blessings He so richly pours out upon us. He does not want us to hide our faith, but instead wants us to openly tell others of the blessings He graciously gives us daily. We in this country have been given many freedoms: freedom to live where we wish, work for whom we choose, associate with anyone we want, and worship where we so desire. Therefore, let us be bold and share our faith openly as God leads us to.

Dwight D. Eisenhower

Almighty God, as we stand here at this moment my future associates in the executive branch of government join me in beseeching that Thou will make full and complete our dedication to the service of the people in this throng, and their fellow citizens everywhere.

Give us, we pray, the power to discern clearly right from wrong, and allow all our words and actions to be governed thereby, and by the laws of this land. Especially we pray that our concern shall be for all the people regardless of station, race, or calling.

May cooperation be permitted and be the mutual aim of those who, under the concepts of our Constitution, hold to differing political faiths; so that all may work for the good of our beloved country and Thy glory. Amen.

—First Act After Receiving the Oath of Office
January 20, 1953

DAY 36

Lord,

We hunger for Your Word. Teach us the way that we should go, and help us walk in Your truth each day. May Your praise always be on our lips, and may You fill our hearts with the joy of Your love and blessing. You are a gracious and loving God whose mercy is new every morning.

Teach me Your way, O Lord;
I will walk in Your truth;
Unite my heart to fear Your name.
I will praise You, O Lord my God, with all my heart,
And I will glorify Your name forevermore.

PSALM 86:11–12

I have declared my ways, and You answered me;
Teach me Your statutes. . . .
Teach me, O LORD, the way of Your statutes,
And I shall keep it to the end.

PSALM 119:26, 33

David asked God to teach him His statutes, and God readily answered his request. Today we would be wise to make the same request of the Almighty. After all, only God can teach us how to make truly wise decisions, how to discern which candidates to vote for, and how to get along with one another after the voting results are in. America is known throughout the world for our patriotism, pride, and honor. Let this be a time of bringing glory and praise to His name while we exercise our freedom of speech and our right to vote during the campaign process and the days to follow.

DAY 37

Father,

We humbly ask for Your blessing. Help us listen to Your counsel when we are alone with You. Speak to our hearts each moment, for You are the anchor of our souls, and we will rest in Your presence. It is You alone we desire; no one and nothing can take Your place.

I will bless the LORD who has given me counsel;
My heart also instructs me in the night seasons.
I have set the LORD always before me;
Because He is at my right hand I shall not be moved.

PSALM 16:7–8

Blessed be the Lord,
Who daily loads us with benefits,
The God of our salvation!

PSALM 68:19

We will never know how much the Lord "loads us with benefits" every day. We don't, for instance, know all that He protects us from. We too easily take for granted many of the blessings we do see—such gifts as food, shelter, friends, family, health, and even life itself. We should find it hard not to praise Him! This truth applies not just to individuals but to our nation as well. Great is God's faithfulness to our straying nation. May God use the prayers prompted by this book to draw our country back to Him. Let us not hesitate to share God's blessings with others and daily serve our risen Savior so that others might know and accept the One who loves us unconditionally.

DAY 38

Lord,

Your Word has given us counsel on how we should relate to and act toward one another. May we be steadfast and immovable in our commitment to You and to one another. Let our roots go deep into Your Word to praise and glorify Your name. May our weakness be Your strength and our purpose in life be to honor You.

Blessed is the man
Who walks not in the counsel of the ungodly,
  Nor stands in the path of sinners,
  Nor sits in the seat of the scornful;
But his delight is in the law of the Lord,
  And in His law he meditates day and night.

PSALM 1:1–2

The counsel of the LORD stands forever,
The plans of His heart to all generations.
Blessed is the nation whose God is the LORD,
The people He has chosen as His own
       inheritance.

PSALM 33:11–12

The word *blessed* appears in the Bible more than seventy times, and on many of those occasions God uses that word to clearly tell us how we—as individuals and as a nation—can be blessed. In each case, God reminds us that all blessings come from Him and that He bestows His blessings on each of us who makes Jesus the Lord of our lives. May this nation come to God—may America make Jesus the Lord of this land—as we humbly ask for His strength and seek His direction.

DAY 39

Lord,

We cry out to You with hearts that need Your blessings. Give us wisdom to make right decisions that will bring honor to You and will purify our hearts. Let the words that we speak draw us closer to Your presence. We recognize, O Lord, that You are in control of all things. Help this nation to hear Your voice, protect us from evil, and lead us in the path of righteousness for Your name's sake.

Hear a just cause, O LORD,
Attend to my cry;
Give ear to my prayer which is not from deceitful lips. . . .
Let Your eyes look on the things that are upright. . . .
That my footsteps may not slip.

PSALM 17:1–2, 5

I know also, my God, that You test the heart
and have pleasure in uprightness. As for me,
in the uprightness of my heart I have willingly
offered all these things; and now with joy I have
seen Your people, who are present here to offer
willingly to You.

1 CHRONICLES 29:17

A gain and again in the Scriptures, God hears His people's prayers and acts on their behalf. So why do we hesitate to approach Him? When we live with uprightness in our hearts, coming to God in prayer can become a more natural desire and a more regular, even daily, practice. Let our prayer life be the center of everything we choose to do, especially in the days ahead as we evaluate each candidate running for office. And, on a grander scale, may our nation repent, turn to God, and become a people of prayer.

DAY 40

Lord,

We live in a nation that is free to elect those chosen for public office. We confess that the servants who are chosen are there with Your approval. Let us faithfully support those elected to office, giving honor to their position. Let us help them fulfill the obligation and responsibility for our nation. With prayer and understanding, let us unite ourselves to the one purpose of living a life in which "In God We Trust."

Let every soul be subject to the governing authorities. For there is no authority except from God, and the authorities that exist are appointed by God. . . . Render therefore to all their due: taxes to whom taxes are due, customs to whom customs, fear to whom fear, honor to whom honor.

ROMANS 13:1, 7

"If anyone wills to do His will, he shall know concerning the doctrine, whether it is from God or whether I speak on My own authority. He who speaks from himself seeks his own glory; but He who seeks the glory of the One who sent Him is true, and no unrighteousness is in Him."

JOHN 7:17–18

We live in a country that gives us—among many freedoms—the right to vote for those who govern us and the right to worship the Lord as we choose. These are privileges we should not disregard. Many other countries do not have such freedom! So, as we worship between now and November, may we pray fervently for our nation. And, come Election Day, may each citizen act responsibly as a 21st-century steward of this nation our God-fearing forefathers envisioned and designed.

The Great Awakenings

The First Great Awakening 1735–1745

The Great Awakening was a period in our history when revival spread throughout the colonies and people were drawn to prayer and a greater spiritual experience. This was a time when American colonies were questioning the role of the individual in their Christian walk and their role in society. This was a time of enlightenment, which emphasized the power of each individual to understand the approach to salvation and the power of prayer.

Great men such as Jonathan Edwards and George Whitefield were key Americans who preached for close to ten years in New England colonies with an emphasis on the personal approach to religion. These men helped unify the American colonies and helped the Great Awakening spread through the work of numerous preachers and revivals. This movement fulfilled people's need for reassurance, direction, and religious purpose. People became united in the understanding of their Christian faith and life.

Jonathan Edwards

The Second Great Awakening

The Second Great Awakening was a Christian revival movement during the early nineteenth century in the United States. It began around 1800 and gained momentum by 1820. The movement expressed a theology, by which every person could be saved through revivals.

Many converts believed that the awakening heralded a new millennial age. This awakening stimulated the establishment of many reform movements designed to remedy the evils of society before the second coming of Jesus Christ.

During this time in history, church membership soared. The Methodist circuit riders and local Baptist preachers made enormous gains. In the newly settled frontier regions, the revival was implemented through camp meetings. Each camp meeting was a religious service of several days' length with multiple preachers.

They were committed to individuals achieving a personal relationship with Jesus Christ.

The Second Great Awakening had a profound impact on American religious history. The membership numbers of the Baptist and Methodists grew dramatically during this period in history. The application of Christian teaching to social problems was commonplace during the early part of the nineteenth century.*

---

*https://en.wikipedia.org/wiki/Second_Great_Awakening

Camp Meeting of the Methodists in N. America

The Third Great Awakening

During the Third Great Awakening, religion played a dominant role in American history. Protestant denominations had a strong sense of social activism. They developed the postmillennial theology that the second coming of Christ would come after the entire earth had been reformed. Social issues gained momentum from the awakening, as did the worldwide missionary movement.

This was a time in history that the mainline Protestant churches were rapidly increasing in number. As the numbers grew, so did their wealth and educational levels. Focusing on reaching the unchurched in America and around the world, many built colleges and universities to train the next generation. In society, the role of a missionary was held in high regard.

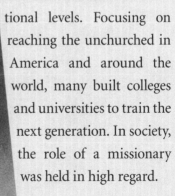

Charles Finney

Photo & Illustration Credits

Notes